Weekly Reader Books presents

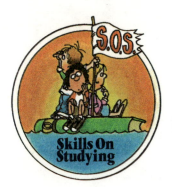

HELP IS ON
THE WAY
FOR:

Maps & Globes

Written by Marilyn Berry
Pictures by Bartholomew

Living Skills Productions
Fallbrook, California

Weekly Reader Books offers several exciting
card and activity programs. For information,
write to WEEKLY READER BOOKS, P.O. Box 16636,
Columbus, Ohio 43216.

Executive Producer: Marilyn Berry
Editor: Theresa Tinkle
Consultants: Patricia Harrington and Terie Snyder
Design: Abigail Johnston
Typesetting: Curt Chelin

For a complete catalog of other living skills materials,
write to: Institute of Living Skills
P.O. Box 1461, Fallbrook, CA 92028

Weekly Reader Books edition published by
arrangement with Living Skills Press.

So you need to learn about **maps and globes.**

Hang on! Help is on the way!

If you are having a hard time

- finding places on a map,
- understanding the parts of a map,
- using an atlas or a gazetteer...

...you are not alone!

Just in case you're wondering...

...why don't we start at the beginning?

What Are Maps and Globes?

Maps are drawings or pictures of the earth. Some include the entire surface of the earth. Others show only a small section of the earth's surface. There are also maps and globes of outer space and of imaginary places.

Why Are Maps and Globes Important?

Maps and globes offer a wealth of information in a simple, easy-to-read form. There will be many occasions when you will find maps and globes useful. Here are some examples:

- Giving directions

- Planning trips

- Understanding current events

Looking for information on a map or globe is like going on a treasure hunt. Finding the information can be fun and easy when you learn how to use all the clues. The key is to take it one step at a time.

Globes

A globe is a map that is shaped like a ball. It is the only type of map that can show you the whole earth's surface in its true shape. A globe is a good type of map to use when you want to
- look at a map of the whole world in its real form,
- see where one place is in relation to the rest of the world, or
- see how the earth is tilted and how it rotates.

Locating Places on the Globe

A globe is divided into sections by imaginary lines.

- The horizontal lines that run east and west are called **parallels of latitude.**
- The vertical lines that run north and south are called **meridians of longitude.**
- When all the lines are drawn, they form the **global grid.** This grid makes it possible for us to transfer information from a globe onto a flat map. It also makes it possible for us to locate points on a globe and measure the distance between them.

The Parallels of Latitude

The parallels of latitude are horizontal lines used to measure distance north and south. They are called "parallels" because they are always the same distance apart. There are five major parallels of latitude.

- **The Equator** circles the earth at its widest point, and divides it into the northern and southern hemispheres.
- **The Tropic of Cancer** and the **Arctic Circle** are between the Equator and the North Pole.
- **The Tropic of Capricorn** and the **Antarctic Circle** are between the Equator and the South Pole.

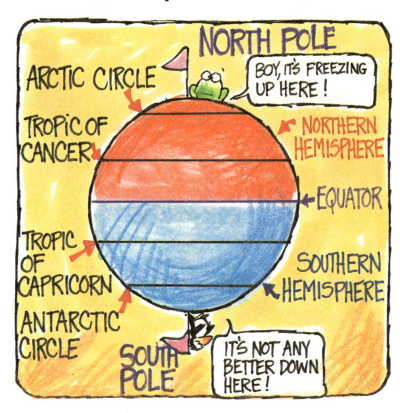

Parallels of latitude are numbered in units called *degrees*. the number of degrees tells how far each line is from the Equator. Here is how the numbering system works:

- The Equator is the center of the earth, so it is labelled 0 degrees.
- The North Pole is 90 degrees north of the Equator.
- The South Pole is 90 degrees south of the Equator.
- All other parallels of latitude fall in between.

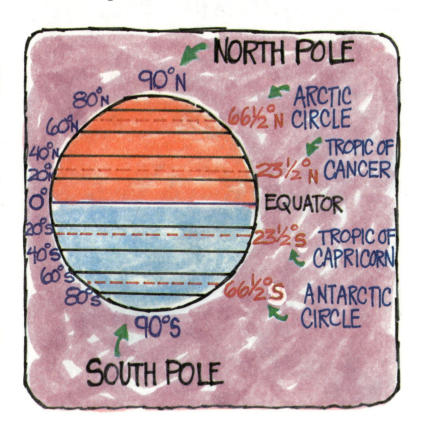

The Meridians of Longitude

The meridians of longitude are vertical lines that are used to measure distance east and west. They are not parallel as are the latitude lines. As the meridians of longitude approach the Poles, they fall closer together. There are two major meridians of longitude.

- **The Prime Meridian** runs from the North Pole through Greenwich, England and then to the South Pole. It divides the earth into the eastern hemisphere and the western hemisphere.
- **The International Date Line** runs from the North Pole through the Pacific Ocean and then to the South Pole. It falls on the opposite side of the earth from the Prime Meridian.

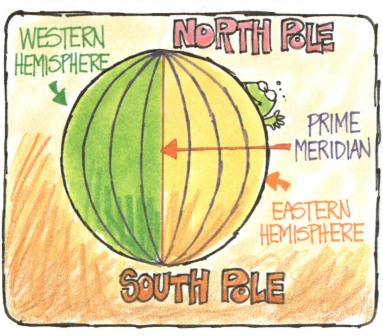

Meridians of longitude lines are also numbered in degrees. However, the number of degrees on meridians of longitude tells how far each line is from the Prime Meridian. Here is how the numbering system works:

- The Prime Meridian is the starting point, so it is labelled 0 degrees.
- The International Date Line is exactly halfway around the earth, so it is labelled 180 degrees.
- All other meridians of longitude fall in between on either the east side or the west side.

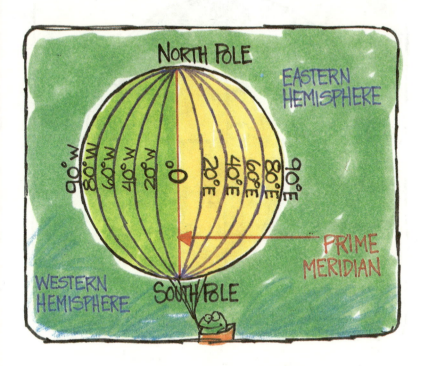

With both latitude and longitude lines drawn on the globe, you have the framework for locating any place on earth. Practice using latitude and longitude lines by finding the place where 40 degrees south and 20 degrees east cross. (Hint: The place is marked with an *.)

Maps

Maps do not have the bulky shape of a globe. Maps are flat and are much more convenient to carry and store. Maps also offer many other kinds of information. There are three different types of maps:

- Physical maps
- Political maps
- Special purpose maps

Physical Maps

Physical maps show the natural features of the earth's surface. They show the different forms of the land such as mountains and valleys. They also show water formations such as rivers, lakes, and streams. There are two types of physical maps: **relief maps** and **topographical maps**.

- **Relief maps** show the appearance of the earth's surface. Color and shading are used to point out the different land and water formations. Some relief maps actually have a raised surface to emphasize the texture of the earth.

- **Topographical maps** show the earth's surface by using *contour lines*. A contour line shows the height of the land. All of the land along one contour line is the same height. This type of map is not colorful, but it is a good way to show how flat or steep the land is. Here are two important tips that will help you read contour lines:

1. When the lines appear far apart, the land is flat.
2. When the lines appear close together, the land is steep.

Political Maps

Political maps offer a different type of information. They show the boundaries continents, countries, states, counties, cities, and towns. Political maps often use color to show how the land is divided. Since boundaries can change, it's a good idea to check the date on a political map to make sure you are getting current information.

Special Purpose Maps

Special purpose maps offer a variety of information. The titles will usually tell you the kind of information you will find on this type of map. Here are some examples of special purpose maps:

- weather maps
- population maps
- natural resources maps
- products maps
- time zone maps
- road maps

It is also a good idea to check the date of special purpose maps to make sure the information is current.

Locating Places on a Map

You can usually locate a place on a map by using one of two different methods.

1. **Using latitude and longitude.** Some maps are marked with a grid of latitude and longitude. The degrees of latitude are listed down the side of the map. The degrees of longitude are listed across the top or bottom of the map. If you know the latitude and longitude of a place, you can locate it on the map by finding the point where the two lines cross.

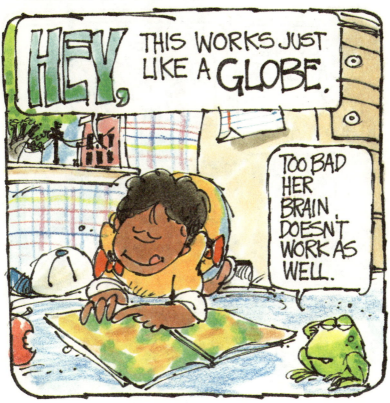

2. **Using a map index.** Some maps have an index that lists all the places that can be found on the map. The places are listed in alphabetical order, and each one is followed by a letter and a number. The letter and number are to be used as a guide for finding the place you want.

How To Use an Index

- Look in the index and find the place you want to locate on the map.
- Read the letter and number printed next to the place and write them on a piece of paper.
- Along one side of the map you will find a column of letters. Find the letter you need.
- Along the top of the map you will find a row of numbers. Find the number you need.
- Draw an imaginary line with your finger across the row. Then draw a second imaginary line down the column.
- Where the two lines cross, you will find the place you are looking for.

Map and Globe Skills

Being able to locate a place on a map or globe is an important skill. However, there are three other skills that are also important.

- Understanding directions
- Using the scale
- Using the key

Understanding Directions

There are four main directions that are used with maps. They are: north, south, east, and west. They are called **cardinal directions**. Sometimes the cardinal directions are combined to make **intermediate directions**. The intermediate directions are: northwest, northeast, southwest, and southeast.

In order to read a map correctly, you need to know how the directions are arranged. On most maps

- North is at the top,
- South is at the bottom,
- East is on the right, and
- West is on the left.

Most maps have a symbol that shows the directions. The symbol is either a *compass rose,* which shows all four directions, or an arrow that points north. This symbol is especially helpful when the top of the map points in a direction other than north. It's always a good idea to check the direction symbol, just to make sure you understand which way the map faces.

Using the Scale

It would be impossible to draw everything on a map in its actual size. Therefore, maps are miniature versions of real places. This is called "drawing to scale."

A map can be either a large-scale picture of an area or a small-scale picture of the same area.

- **Large-scale maps** cover a small section of land but show a great amount of detail.

- **Small-scale maps** cover a much larger area of land but show very little detail.

A map scale helps you measure the actual distance between two points on a map. The scale can be stated in three different ways. For example:

- In words: 1 inch represents 100 miles.
- As a ratio: 1: 100 or 1/100.
- As a sample: |_____|

  100 miles .

LET'S SEE...
ONE INCH EQUALS
100 MILES AND
IT'S THREE AND
A HALF INCHES...
THAT MAKES IT
350 MILES TO
THE BORDER.

HMMM

FROGS
DON'T
HAVE
SCALES.

There are two ways to measure distance
on a map.

- **Direct distance** is the shortest distance between
  two points. It is easily measured with a ruler.
- **Road distance** is always greater than direct
  distance. It is also more difficult to measure
  because the roads do not follow a straight line.

Using the Key

A map key (sometimes called a legend) explains how the information is displayed on a map. It is usually located in one of the lower corners of the map. Maps use many different symbols for displaying information. To get the most out of a map, you will need to look at the key and become familiar with its symbols.

Picture symbols are used a lot on special purpose maps for showing information such as:

- Road signs
- Natural resources
- Weather
- Landmarks

Color is used on all types of maps to show different kinds of information. Color is used on
- political maps to show the areas of different countries or states,
- physical maps to show the different textures of the earth's surface, and on
- special purpose maps to show information such as quantities.

Where to Find Maps

There are many different places where you can find a variety of maps. Here are just a few:

- The library (look in the card catalog under the name of the place)
- Travel agencies
- Automobile clubs
- Gas stations

There are also many different resources that contain maps such as:

- Atlases
- Encyclopedias
- Books about travel
- Magazines
- Newspapers

Using an Atlas

An atlas is a collection of maps that are bound together to form a book. Many atlases include:

- Information about how to use an atlas and general facts about maps
- Photographs, drawings, tables, and graphs
- Articles that give facts about such things as climate, population, and history
- A glossary of terms

There are many different atlases available. When you are looking for an atlas, keep these things in mind:

- Look at the date of publication. You want to make sure the atlas is up-to-date.
- Look to see what types of maps are included.
- Look at the introductory material. Make sure the instructions for using the atlas are clear and easy to follow.

Using a Gazetteer

A gazetteer is a dictionary of geography that lists places around the world. Instead of using maps, the gazetteer gives brief descriptions about each place. The information usually includes:

- The location of the place
- The correct pronunciation of the place's name
- What the place is, such as a town, country, or river
- A brief description
- Historical information

Making a Map

Now that you know how to read a map, you can try making your own. If you start out by making a simple map, you will see how easy and fun it can be. You will need to follow three simple steps, and you will need

- unlined paper,
- a lead pencil with an eraser,
- a ruler, and
- colored pencils or pens.

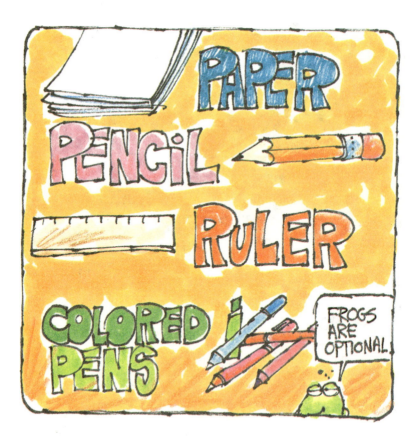

Step One: Decide on the purpose of your map.
Before you begin drawing your map, you need to answer some important questions.

- What information do you want your map to show?
- What area do you want to include in your map?
- What type of map will best display the information?

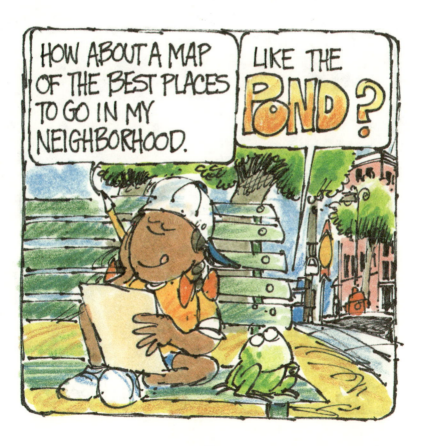

Step Two: Draw the basic outline of your map.
Now it is time to begin drawing your map. To start, use a lead pencil with an eraser so you can make changes and corrections as you work.

- Decide on the scale you will use and write it down in the bottom corner of your map.
- Determine the direction of your map and draw a symbol that shows which way your map will face.
- Draw the area that is included in your map.

Step Three: Complete your map.

The final step is to plot the information on your map. Record the information in lead pencil and then color the map with your colored pencils or pens.

- Decide how to display the information. Decide if you want to use picture symbols or just colors. Plot the information on your map.
- Make a legend or key and draw in the symbols and their explanations.
- Make an index if necessary.

2" = 1 block

▢ = Big Screen TV.

🍕 = Great Snacks

◖ = Video Games

☠ = Makes you Work

= Good place to play

☺ = Swimming pool

If you follow the suggestions in this book...

...you will discover a whole new world!

THE END

About the Author

Marilyn Berry has a master's degree in education with a specialization in reading. She is on staff as a creator of supplementary materials at Living Skills Press. Marilyn and her husband Steve Patterson have two sons, John and Brent.

Weekly Reader Books presents

HELP IS ON THE WAY FOR:

Charts & Graphs

Written by Marilyn Berry
Pictures by Bartholomew

Living Skills Productions
Fallbrook, California

Weekly Reader Books offers several exciting
card and activity programs. For information,
write to WEEKLY READER BOOKS, P.O. Box 16636,
Columbus, Ohio 43216.

Executive Producer: Marilyn Berry
Editor: Theresa Tinkle
Consultants: Patricia Harrington and Terie Snyder
Design: Abigail Johnston
Typesetting: Curt Chelin

For a complete catalog of other living skills materials,
write to: Institute of Living Skills
P.O. Box 1461, Fallbrook, CA 92028

Weekly Reader Books edition published by
arrangement with Living Skills Press.

So you need to learn about **charts and graphs?**

Hang on! Help is on the way.

If you are having a hard time

- reading charts and graphs,
- knowing which types of charts and graphs to use, or
- making charts and graphs...

...you are not alone!

Just in case you're wondering...

...why don't we start at the beginning?

What Are Charts and Graphs?

Charts and graphs are drawings or diagrams that present information in a quick, easy-to-read form. Charts and graphs allow you to record a lot of information in a small amount of space.

Why Are Charts and Graphs Important?

We get information from many different sources such as:
- books
- newspapers
- magazines
- television

These sources often use charts and graphs to present some of their information. To understand all the information each source offers, you need to be able to read the charts and graphs.

It is also important for you to know how to make your own charts and graphs.

You will find that charts and graphs can be helpful tools for

- Your personal use

- Your schoolwork

Charts and graphs are like puzzles. You need to figure out what pieces of information are involved and how they fit together.

There are simple formulas you can follow for both reading and making charts and graphs. It can be fun if you just take it one step at a time.

9

Charts

There are two different types of charts. Each type serves a different purpose.

Tables and Schedules

Tables and schedules list information that can be used over and over as a reference such as:
• a table of multiplication facts, or
• a bus schedule.

The information is listed in columns (that you read from top to bottom) and rows (that you read from left to right).

The parts of a table or schedule are:

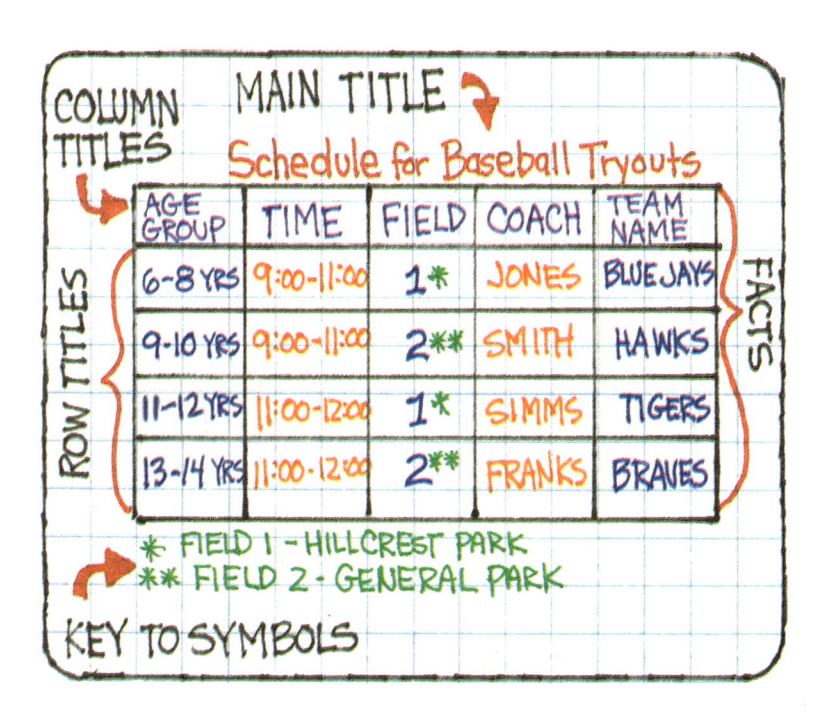

COLUMN TITLES
MAIN TITLE
Schedule for Baseball Tryouts

ROW TITLES

FACTS

AGE GROUP	TIME	FIELD	COACH	TEAM NAME
6-8 YRS	9:00-11:00	1*	JONES	BLUE JAYS
9-10 YRS	9:00-11:00	2**	SMITH	HAWKS
11-12 YRS	11:00-12:00	1*	SIMMS	TIGERS
13-14 YRS	11:00-12:00	2**	FRANKS	BRAVES

* FIELD 1 - HILLCREST PARK
** FIELD 2 - GENERAL PARK

KEY TO SYMBOLS

Practice using this chart by finding the name of the field where a 12-year-old would go for baseball tryouts.

- Slide your finger down the row titles until you come to the row entitled "11-12 yrs."
- Slide your finger across that row until you reach the column entitled "Field."
- Your finger will be pointing to "1*."
- Look up the symbol (*) in the "Key to Symbols" and you will find the name of the field. The answer is Field 1 at Hillcrest Park.

Progress Charts

Progress charts are used to record information as it is gathered. Some examples are:

- a schoolwork progress chart,
- a weather chart, and
- an expenses chart.

This type of chart is drawn with only the main title, the row titles, and the column titles filled in at the beginning. The rest of the information is filled in as it happens.

The parts of a progress chart are:

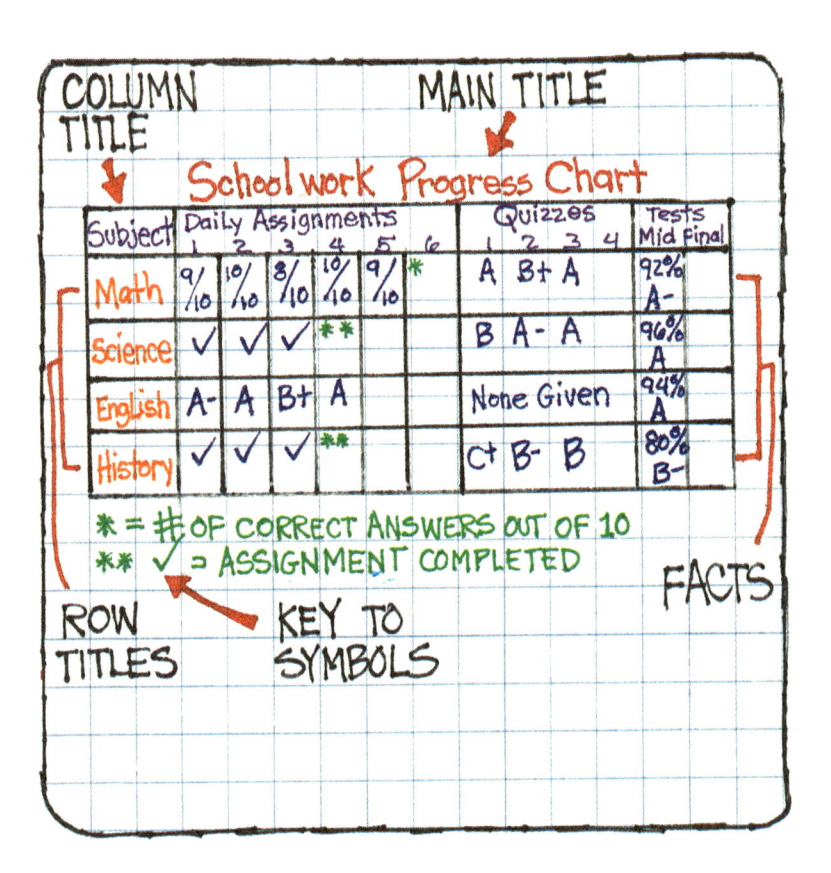

Practice using the chart by finding the grade that was given for the English test.

- Slide your finger down the row titles until you come to the row entitled "English."
- Slide your finger across that row until you reach the column entitled "Tests."
- Your finger will be pointing to "94% A," which is the answer.

Making Your Own Chart

You can make your own chart by following four simple steps.

Step One: Decide which type of chart you need.

- You will want to make a **table or schedule** if you have information that you need to organize, and will use over and over.
- You will want to make a **progress chart** if you need to gather information, and record the information as it happens.

Step Two: Decide on the basic parts of your chart.

- Begin with the title. Ask yourself, "What do I hope to learn from this chart?"
- Decide on the main ingredients. You will need to decide on the column titles and the row titles. You can usually find these ingredients suggested in the main title. For example:
Title—"After-School Time Chart."
Ingredients—School *days* and after school *hours.*

Step Three: Draw your chart.

You will need
- graph paper,
- a ruler, and
- a pencil.

Instructions:
- Count the number of column titles you need and draw that many columns on your paper.
- Count the number of row titles you need and draw that many rows on your paper.
- Fill in the proper column and row titles.
- Write the title of your chart at the top of the page.

16

Step Four: Fill in the facts on your chart.
If you are making a table or schedule, you can fill in the facts on your chart immediately. For example, for an "After-School Time Chart" you would

- make a plan for the best use of your time (include activities that are already planned such as dinner and chores),
- record your plan by filling in the facts on the chart, then
- use the chart as a guide for spending your time.

COLUMN TITLES → MAIN TITLE ↓

After School Time Chart

HOURS	Mon.	Tues.	Wed.	Thurs.	Fri.
3-3:30	Relax	Relax	Relax	Relax	Relax
3:30-4	Piano	Practice	Practice	Practice	Practice
4-4:30					
4:30-5					
5-5:30		Soccer		Soccer	
5:30-6	Drama		Drama		Drama
6-6:30	Dinner	Dinner	Dinner	Dinner	Dinner
6:30-7	Dishes	Dishes	Dishes	Dishes	Dishes
7-7:30					
7:30-8					
8-8:30	Freetime	Freetime	Freetime	Freetime	Freetime
8:30-9	Bedtime	Bedtime	Bedtime	Bedtime	Bedtime

← ROW TITLES

FACTS →

KEY: //// AVAILABLE STUDY TIME

↑ KEY TO SYMBOLS

17

If you are making a progress chart, you will not fill the chart in all at once. Instead, you will fill in the facts as they happen. To be completely accurate, you may want to keep your chart with you and record your activities at the end of each hour. Once your chart is completed, you will have gathered a lot of interesting information.

Many times there will be more information in a chart than you see at first glance. For example, an "After-School Time Chart" can tell you
• how much total time is spent on each activity, and
• how the time spent on one activity compares with the time spent on a different activity.

Another way to find this out is to put the information on a graph.

Graphs

There are four different types of graphs:
- the line graph,
- the bar graph,
- the circle graph, and
- the pictograph.

Each type of graph serves a different purpose and displays information in a different way. Here are examples of each type of graph:

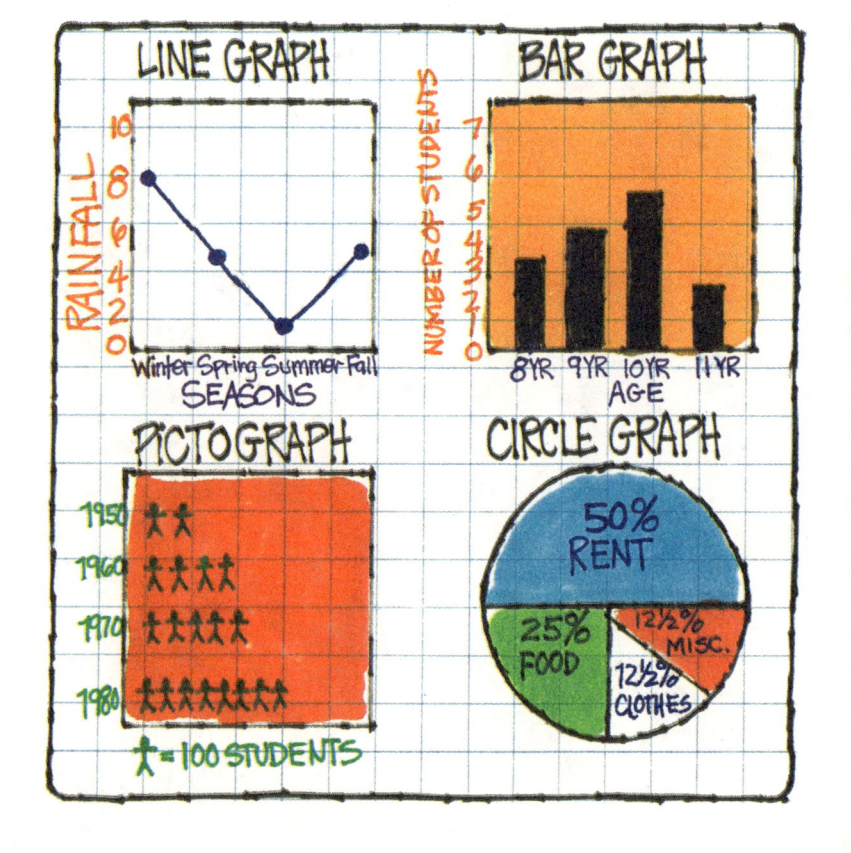

How to Read Graphs

There are three different types of information you will need to look for when reading a graph.

1. **The general information** gives you an overview of what you can expect to find in the graph.
2. **The specific information** includes the actual information that is plainly stated in the graph.
3. **The suggested information** is information not actually stated in the graph but is "suggested" by the other information.

Reading a Line Graph

The line graph is one of the easiest graphs to read. It is especially useful for showing change over a period of time.

1. The general information. For an overview of the line graph, you need to study its basic parts.

- Read the main title. This tells you what the graph is about.
- Read the titles on the vertical axis (the line running from top to bottom).
- Read the titles on the horizontal axis (the line running from left to right).
- Read the source of information. This tells you how reliable the information is.
- Read the key to the symbols. This tells you how the symbols are used in the graph.

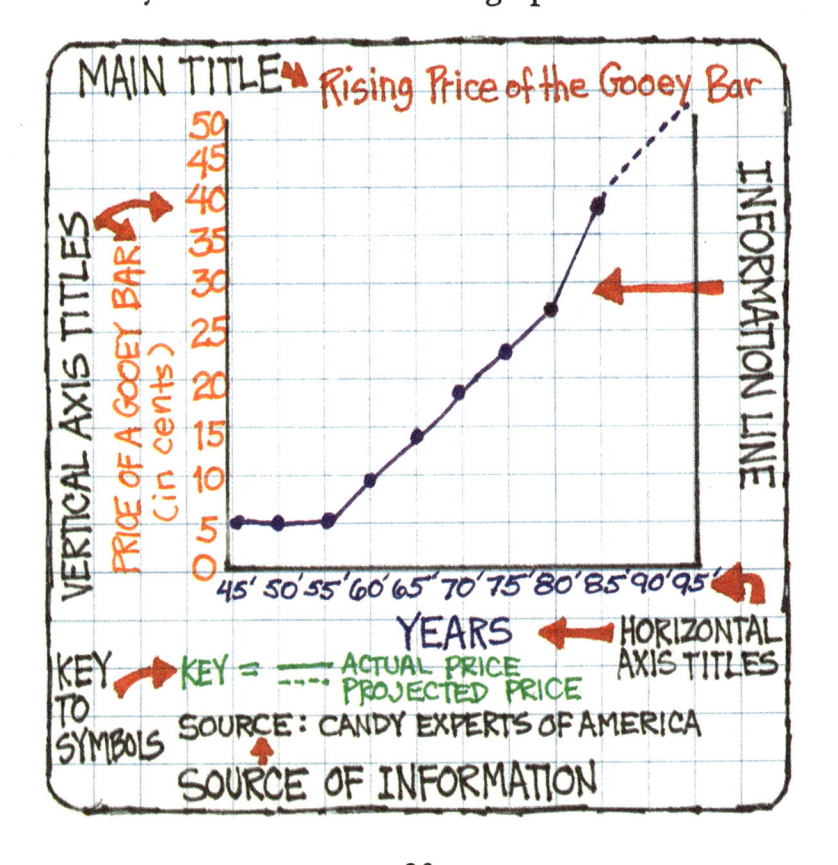

2. The specific information is found on the information line. Practice using the information line by finding the price of a Gooey Bar in 1965.

- Slide your finger along the horizontal axis until you come to the title "1965."
- Slide your finger straight up until you reach the information line.
- Slide your finger to the left until you reach the vertical axis.
- Your finger will be pointing to the answer, which is 15 cents.

3. The suggested information. You can practice looking for suggested information by studying the graph on page 23 and asking questions such as:

- How has the price of a Gooey Bar changed since 1950? *Answer:* The price has increased.
- If the change that is shown on the chart continues, what will happen? *Answer:* The price will continue to increase.

Reading a Bar Graph

The bar graph is also a simple graph to read. This type of graph is especially useful for comparing information.

1. The general information. For an overview of the bar graph, you need to study its basic parts.

- Read the main title. What is the graph about?
- Read the vertical and horizontal axis titles. What kinds of information are presented?
- Read the source of information. Is it reliable?
- Read the key to the symbols. How are the symbols used?

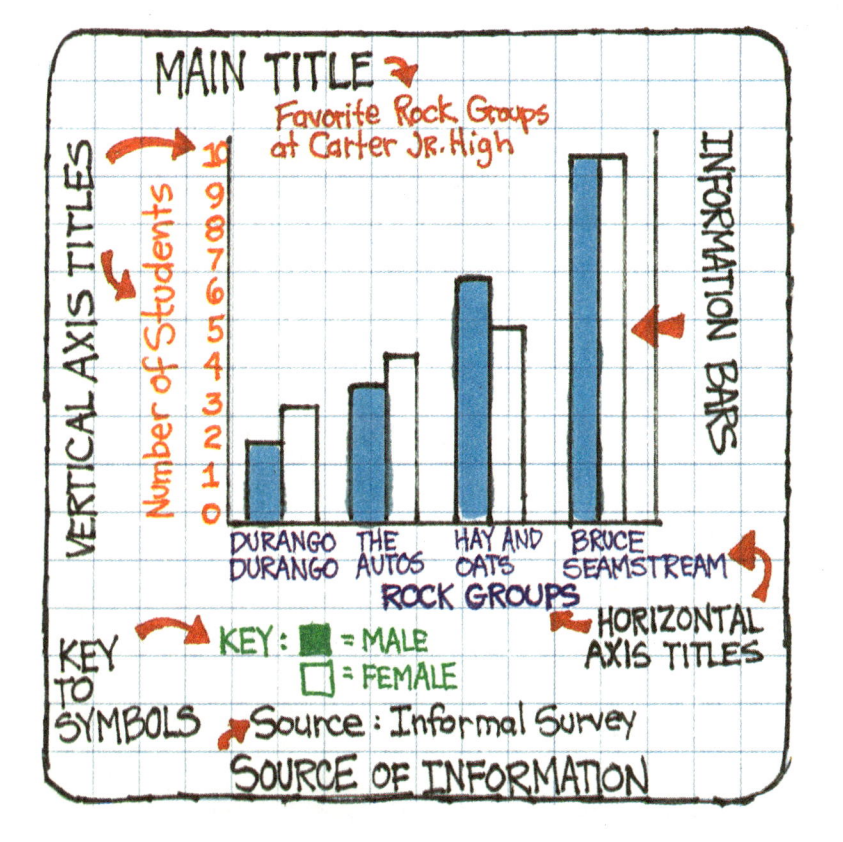

2. The specific information is found in the
information bars. Practice using the information
bars by finding the number of males who chose
"The Autos" as the best rock group.

- Slide your finger along the horizontal axis until
  you come to the title "The Autos."
- Using the key, find the bar that represents males.
- Slide your finger up to the top of the bar.
- Slide your finger to the left until you reach the
  vertical axis.
- Your finger will be pointing to the answer,
  which is 4 males.

3. The suggested information. You can practice looking for suggested information by studying the graph on page 27 and asking questions such as:

- Who would probably sell the most records at Carter Jr. High? *Answer:* Bruce Seamstream.
- Is there a big difference in musical taste between the girls and the boys? *Answer:* No. The tastes seem to be very similar.

Reading a Pictograph

The pictograph can be a fun type of graph to read. Instead of using bars to represent the information, the pictograph uses pictures or symbols. It is also used to compare information.

1. The general information. For an overview of the pictograph, you need to study its basic parts.

- Read the main title. What is the graph about?
- Read the vertical axis titles. What kind of information is presented?
- Read the key to the symbols. How are the symbols used?
- Read the source of the information. Is it reliable?

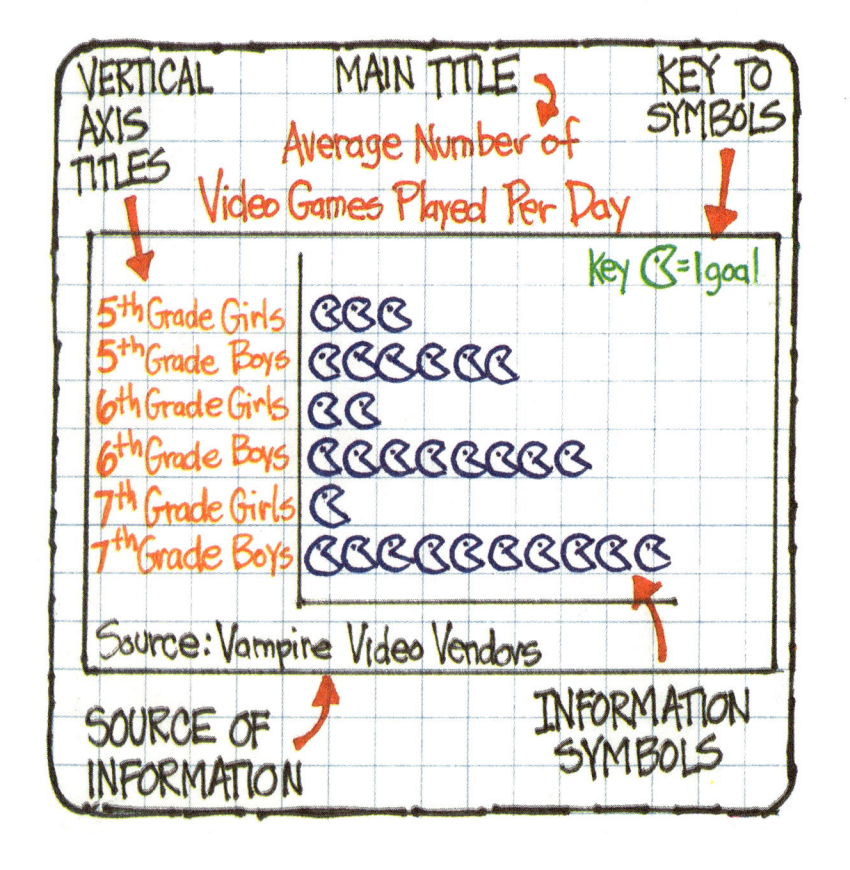

2. The specific information is found in the information symbols. Practice using the information symbols by finding the average number of video games 7th grade boys play per day.

- Slide your finger down the vertical axis until you come to the title "7th Grade Boys."
- Slide your finger to the right and count the symbols in the row.
- Multiply the number of symbols (10) by the value of the symbol in the key (1): 10 × 1 = 10. *Answer:* The 7th grade boys play an average of 10 games a day.

3. The suggested information. You can practice looking for suggested information by studying the graph on page 31 and asking questions such as:

- Who plays more video games—girls or boys? *Answer:* According to this graph—boys.
- What changes take place as the girls and boys get older? *Answer:* The girls play less, and the boys play more.

Reading a Circle Graph

The circle graph is sometimes called a pie graph. This type of graph is especially useful when you need to show how a whole is divided into parts. Circle graphs are usually based on percentages.

- The whole circle = 100%
- Each segment is assigned a percentile value. The size of the segment is drawn to match that percentile.
- All the segments must add up to 100%

1. The general information. For an overview of the circle graph, you need to study its basic parts.

- Read the main title. What is the graph about?
- Read the segment titles. What does each part of the circle stand for?

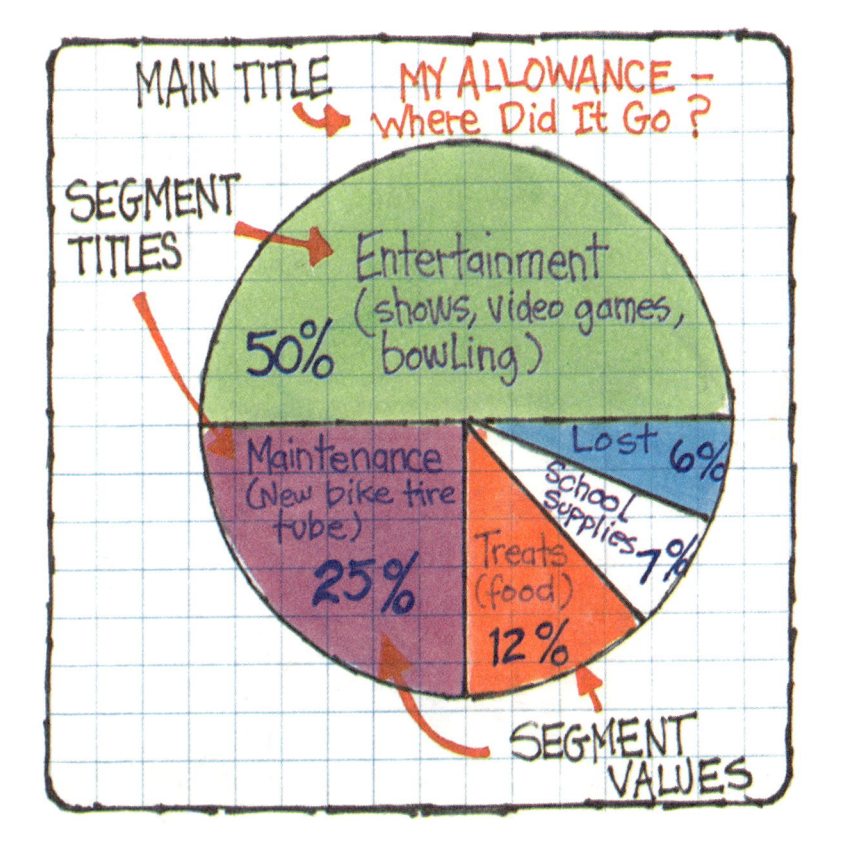

2. The specific information. Locating the specific information on a circle graph is easy. Simply read each segment title and identify the value assigned to each segment. You can practice by finding out how much of the allowance was spent on entertainment.

• Locate the segment entitled "Entertainment."
• Look at the percentile assigned to that segment. *Answer:* 50% of the allowance was spent on entertainment.

3. The suggested information. You can practice looking for suggested information by studying the graph on page 35 and asking questions such as:

- What was most of the allowance spent on?
  Answer: Entertainment.
- How much money was put into savings?
  Answer: None.

Making Your Own Graphs

To make most graphs you will need
- graph paper,
- a ruler, and
- a pencil.

You can make your own graph by following these simple steps.

Step One: Decide which type of graph you need.
- If you want to show change over a period of time, make a line graph.
- If you want to compare information, make a bar graph or a pictograph.
- If you need to show how a "whole" is divided into "segments," make a circle graph.

Step Two: Decide on the basic parts of your graph.

- Begin with the title. "Ask yourself, "What major question will my graph answer?"
- Next, gather the information. Ask yourself, "What information do I need in order to complete my graph?"
- Divide the information into two categories, or sets. This will help you plot the information on your graph.

Step Three: Draw your graph.

Instructions for making a line graph:
- Study one set of information. Figure out the title for your horizontal axis ("game number") and plot the game numbers on your graph.
- Study the other set of information. Figure out the title for your vertical axis ("number of goals scored") and plot the numbers on your graph.
- Record the information at the proper points on your graph and connect the points with a line. For example, above the first game, put a point at the "2." This shows they scored two goals during the first game.

INFORMATION
Number of Goals
Scored Each Game

GAME #	# of Goals
1	2
2	1
3	2
4	3
5	4
6	4
7	5
8	6
9	

LINE GRAPH
Number of Goals
Scored Each Game

THEY'VE IMPROVED!

Instructions for making a bar graph:

- Study one set of information. Figure out the title for your horizontal axis ("game number") and plot the game numbers on your graph.
- Study the other set of information. Figure out the title for your vertical axis ("number of goals scored") and plot the numbers on your graph.
- Record the information at the proper points on your graph as you did on the line graph. However, instead of connecting the points with a line, fill in the column under each point to form a bar.

INFORMATION

Number of Goals
Scored Each Game

GAME #	# of Goals
1	2
2	1
3	2
4	3
5	4
6	5
7	4
8	5
9	6

BAR GRAPH

Number of Goals
Scored Each Game

GAME NUMBER

Instructions for making a pictograph:

- Choose which set of information you want to illustrate with symbols (number of goals scored).
- Select a symbol and decide on its value. Record the symbol and the value in the key. For example, you might use one soccer ball to stand for one goal.
- Study the other set of information. Figure out the titles for your vertical axis and plot them on your graph (list of games by number).
- Record the information by drawing the proper number of symbols in each row.

INFORMATION

⬇

Number of Goals Scored Each Game

Game	# of Goals Scored
1st	1
2nd	2
3rd	3
4th	4
5th	5
6th	4

PICTOGRAPH

⬇

Number of Goals Scored Each Game

Key ⊗ = 1 Goal

Game #1	⊗
Game #2	⊗⊗
Game #3	⊗⊗⊗
Game #4	⊗⊗⊗⊗
Game #5	⊗⊗⊗⊗⊗
Game #6	⊗⊗⊗⊗

I LIKE THIS ONE BEST.

Instructions for making a circle graph:
A circle graph is a little more difficult to make. It takes some extra supplies as well as some extra figuring. You will need

- a percentage protractor (it's much easier to use than a regular protractor),
- a compass,
- paper,
- a ruler, and
- a pencil.

Start as you would with the other graphs.

- Begin with the title. Ask yourself, "What major question will my circle graph answer?" For example, you might want to find out how you spend your time. Your title might be "My 24-Hour Day."
- Gather the information and divide it into segments.
- Assign each segment a value.
- Change the value into a percentage.

MY 24-HOUR DAY

Segment Title	Value (in hours)	Value (in percentages)
Body Maintenance *	12 HRS.	50%
School	6 HRS.	25%
Chores Homework	3 HRS	12 1/2%
Free time	3 HRS	12 1/2%
* Eating Sleeping Exercising		

WHAT A LiFE!

Now it's time to draw your circle graph.

- Draw a circle with the compass. Make sure it is large enough to hold all your segment titles.
- Place the percentage protractor over the circle and mark the percentages for each segment.
- Using the ruler, draw the lines for the segments according to your marks.
- Label each segment with the proper title and value.

If you try the ideas in this book, you will be able to *read* and *make* charts and graphs...

...you might even have fun doing it!

THE END

About the Author

Marilyn Berry has a master's degree in education with a specialization in reading. She is on staff as a creator of supplementary materials at Living Skills Press. Marilyn and her husband Steve Patterson have two sons, John and Brent.